I0505277

FROM ZERO TO ONE

Achieving Unprecedented Success in a World of Constant Change

Frank T. Lester

Copyright © by Frank T. Lester 2023. All rights reserved.

Before this document is duplicated or reproduced in any manner, the publisher's consent must be gained. Therefore, the contents within can neither be stored electronically, transferred, nor kept in a database. Neither in part nor full can the document be copied, scanned, faxed or retained without approval from the publisher or creator.

Table of Contents

Introduction

The world we live in today is full of unprecedented opportunities and challenges. We have unprecedented access to technology, resources, and information that can enable us to create and innovate. There isn't just one equation for success, though. Every journey to success is unique and requires a different approach. In "From Zero to One: Achieving Unprecedented Success in a World of Constant Change," author Frank T. Lester provides a comprehensive guide to help you succeed in your unique journey. Through his experience as a business leader, entrepreneur, and investor, Lester outlines the principles, strategies, and tactics you need to understand and apply to reach success. He guides you through the process of turning your dreams into reality, from the first spark of an idea to the ultimate goal of success. With his insight, you will learn how to develop a winning strategy, how to focus on what matters most, how to make the most of your resources, and how to stay motivated and inspired along the way. By the end of this book, you will have the knowledge, skills, and confidence to take your life and career to the next level.

Chapter 1

The Challenge of the Future

The challenge of the future is likely to be one of unprecedented complexity. The world is already facing a wide range of interrelated challenges, from climate change and resource shortages to economic inequality and the rise of artificial intelligence. To meet these challenges, we must develop new ways of thinking and acting, and find innovative solutions that benefit all of humanity.

Innovations in technology, especially the development of artificial intelligence (AI) and the Internet of Things (IoT), are driving rapid change in the world. They are transforming how we work, live and interact, creating both opportunities and challenges. At the same time, global economic, political, and social forces are creating a more interconnected, interdependent, and unpredictable world.

To meet these challenges, we need to think and act in new ways. We must be more creative, collaborative, and innovative in our approach to problem-solving. We need to embrace the power of technology and use it to create new solutions and address existing challenges. We must also become more conscious of our responsibilities as global citizens, and work together to ensure a more equitable and sustainable future for all. Furthermore, we must also recognize that the future is unpredictable and that our actions today will have an impact on the world tomorrow. We must be prepared to adapt to changing circumstances and look for ways to mitigate the risks and maximize the opportunities presented by a rapidly changing world. The challenge of the future is to be prepared to respond to the challenges of today while laying the groundwork for a better tomorrow.

Chapter 2

Companies as Machines for Creating Value

Companies can be thought of as machines for creating value. They are complex systems that take inputs of resources and labor, process them, and produce outputs of products, services, and profits. Companies use a variety of strategies to increase value and maximize profits, such as building strong customer relationships, leveraging economies of scale, and investing in research and development.

Companies are comprised of people, processes, and technology. The people within a company are the most important factor in creating value. They are the ones who actually create the products and services, manage the operations, and lead the company forward. Processes are the systems and procedures that enable the company to efficiently create value. Technology is the tools and platforms used to enable people and processes to be as effective as possible.

A successful company will have a strong focus on creating value for its customers and stakeholders. This means that the products and services must be of high quality and meet the needs of customers. Companies must also focus on providing the best possible customer service, as this will help to build a loyal customer base. Additionally, companies must find ways to increase efficiency and reduce costs to maximize profits.

Companies are constantly evolving and adapting to changes in the market. They must stay on top of trends and invest in the right areas to ensure that they remain competitive. Companies must also have the flexibility to pivot when the market demands it. To remain profitable and create long-term value, companies must continuously innovate and strive to stay ahead of the competition.

In short, companies are machines for creating value. They combine people, processes, and technology to produce products and services that meet customer needs and generate profits. Companies must also continuously adapt and innovate to stay competitive and remain profitable. By focusing on creating value for customers, companies can ensure their long-term success.

Chapter 3

Network Effects and the New Economy

Network effects play an important role in the new economy, as they refer to the idea that the value of a product or service increases with the number of people using it. This concept has been around for quite some time, but with the advent of the internet and digital technologies, it has become increasingly relevant and useful. Network effects are particularly important in the new economy, as they can help create powerful and sustainable competitive advantages for companies. For example, a business with a large network of customers may be able to charge more for its services than a comparable business with a smaller network, as the larger network will be able to attract more customers and increase demand. Network effects can also be used to create a "winner-take-all" market, where one company dominates the market because of its large customer base.

Network effects can also be used to create economies of scale, as the cost of providing a product or service decreases as more people use it. This can be especially beneficial for companies that offer cloud-based services, as they can benefit from increased scale as more customers join their service.

Finally, network effects can be used to create new business opportunities and markets. For instance, social media platforms such as Facebook and Twitter have been able to leverage network effects to expand their businesses and create entirely new markets.

Overall, network effects are a powerful tool in the new economy and can have a significant impact on a business's success. As such, understanding and leveraging network effects is essential for businesses operating in the digital age.

Chapter 4

How to Design a Business Model

A business model is a framework that outlines the structure of a business and its operations. It describes how a business generates revenue, creates value for its customers, and delivers its products and services. To design a business model, identify the key components of your business, such as the customer, the product or service, the market, the competitive environment, and the operational structure. Then develop a plan to optimize each component and bring them together to create a cohesive business model. Consider factors such as pricing, distribution, customer service, marketing, and technology to create a comprehensive model that defines how your business will create and capture value.

The following are to be considered when designing a business model:

1. Define Your Value Proposition: Determine what your product or service offers that is unique or better than its competitors. This will help you create a competitive advantage and stand out in the market.

2. Identify Your Target Market: Who are the people that will benefit most from your product or service? Research their demographics, needs, and preferences to ensure that you can meet their expectations.

3. Establish Your Revenue Streams: Think of the different ways you can make money from your product or service. Consider pricing models, advertising, and other sources of income.

4. Set Your Costs: Calculate the cost of production, marketing, and other expenses to determine how much you need to charge for your product or service.

5. Determine Your Distribution Channels: Decide how you will get your product or service to the customer. Consider retail stores, online channels, and other options.

6. Develop Your Brand: Create a unique identity for your business. This will help you build an emotional connection and trust with customers.

7. Monitor Your Performance: Track your progress and make adjustments as needed. This will help you stay on top of changing market conditions and customer preferences.

Chapter 5

The Future of Technology

The future of technology is an exciting prospect to consider. As technology advances, it is certain that new and improved technologies will be developed, allowing us to do things we have never been able to do before. Some of the areas that are likely to be impacted by technology in the future include healthcare, education, transportation, and communication.

In the healthcare field, technologies such as artificial intelligence, machine learning, and 3D printing could be used to diagnose and treat diseases in a more precise and efficient manner. Technologies such as virtual reality and augmented reality could also be used to provide better patient care and education.

In the educational field, technology could make learning easier, more engaging, and more accessible. With the help of virtual reality, students could experience a virtual world where they could learn in a more immersive and interactive manner.

In the transportation field, technology could be used to create autonomous vehicles that can safely transport people from one place to another. Autonomous vehicles could also be used in the logistics industry to make deliveries faster and more efficient.

In the communication field, technologies such as 5G, the Internet of Things (IoT), and blockchain could revolutionize the way we communicate with each other. 5G will provide faster and more reliable Internet connections, while IoT will enable devices to communicate with each other over the Internet. Blockchain could be used to make transactions more secure and transparent.

Overall, the future of technology is full of possibilities. As technology continues to evolve, we can expect to see more advances in the fields of healthcare, education, transportation, and communication.

Chapter 6

The Laws of Platforms

Platforms are the backbone of the internet. They provide the infrastructure needed to connect people, services, and products. As such, they have become an increasingly important part of how we interact with the world around us. To ensure the safety, security, and fairness of the services they provide, many platforms have put in place laws and regulations governing their use.

The primary law that applies to platforms is the Communications Decency Act (CDA). This law shields platforms from being liable for the content posted by their users. This means that if a user posts something illegal, the platform is not held responsible. However, the CDA also requires platforms to remove unlawful content, that promotes hatred or violence or is otherwise deemed to be inappropriate. Platforms must also provide users with ways to report inappropriate content and must take appropriate action when such reports are made.

In addition to the CDA, platforms must also comply with a variety of other laws and regulations. These include laws governing privacy, data protection, intellectual property, copyright, and consumer protection, as well as laws related to advertising and marketing. Platforms must also be sure to comply with any local laws that apply in the countries or regions in which they operate.

Finally, platforms must adhere to the terms of service that they have established for their users. These terms of service outline the rules and regulations that apply to the platform and must be followed to maintain the integrity of the platform.

These laws and regulations are intended to ensure that platforms remain safe and secure for their users and that the services they provide remain fair and just. By complying with these laws, platforms can help to ensure that their

users have a positive experience when using
their services.

Chapter 7

Managing Organizational Growth

Managing organizational growth is essential for any business to succeed. It helps to ensure that a company can adjust to changing market conditions and capitalize on opportunities. To successfully manage growth, several important factors need to be taken into consideration. First, it is important to understand the current state of the company and develop a strategy that will enable it to reach its desired level of growth. This requires analyzing current and past performance, understanding customer needs and wants, and establishing a clear vision for the future. It also involves identifying potential markets and creating a plan for how to best reach them.

Once a plan is in place, it is important to focus on execution. This means setting realistic goals and timelines, and consistently tracking performance against them. It also involves developing the necessary resources and capabilities to support the growth plan. This includes recruiting the right people, investing in the necessary infrastructure and equipment, and creating the necessary processes and systems. Finally, it is important to monitor progress and make adjustments as necessary. This involves regularly evaluating performance and making changes to the plan as needed. It is also important to learn from mistakes and use them to inform future decisions.

Overall, managing organizational growth is an essential part of any business. It requires careful planning, execution, and monitoring to ensure that the company can capitalize on opportunities and remain competitive in an ever-changing market.

Chapter 8

The Future of Investing

The future of investing is bright and full of possibilities. The advent of new technologies and the rapid growth of the global economy has created an environment conducive to innovative investment strategies. As the world of investing continues to evolve, there are a variety of opportunities for those interested in exploring new avenues of investing.

One of the most exciting developments in the future of investing is the rise of automated investing. Automated investing, also known as robo-advisors, allows individuals to make investments with little to no manual intervention. Robo-advisors use algorithms to create and manage portfolios that are tailored to the individual's risk tolerance and financial goals. This type of investing promises to make investing more accessible and cost-effective for everyone.

Cryptocurrencies are another exciting new avenue of investing. This digital form of money is becoming increasingly popular, and the potential for investment opportunities is vast. Since cryptocurrencies are decentralized, no single entity has any control over them. This makes them appealing to investors who want to be able to control their investments without interference from a third party.

Another emerging trend in the future of investing is the use of artificial intelligence (AI). AI-driven investment tools are designed to use algorithms to analyze vast amounts of data and identify patterns and trends in the markets. These algorithms can then be used to make decisions about which investments to make. This technology is becoming increasingly popular among institutional investors, but it is also accessible to individual investors who are looking for automated and cost-effective investing strategies.

Finally, investing in socially responsible companies is a growing trend that is likely to continue in the future. Investing in companies that are committed to sustainability, diversity, and corporate responsibility is becoming increasingly popular as investors become more aware of the importance of these issues. Companies that are making a positive impact on the environment and society are likely to perform better in the long term and provide more stable returns for investors.

The future of investing is full of potential and opportunity. As technology continues to evolve and the global economy continues to expand, investors will have access to a greater variety of investment options and strategies. Whether you're looking to invest in traditional assets, cryptocurrencies, AI-driven strategies, or socially responsible companies, the future of investing is sure to be an exciting one.

Chapter 9

The End of Jobs

The Rise of On-Demand Workers and Agile
Corporations is an exploration of the impact of
the Internet and digital technology on the global
labor market. It looks at the various emerging
trends in the job market, such as the rise of the
gig economy, the shift to more flexible
employment models, and the increasing
prevalence of automation and artificial
intelligence. The book examines how these
changes are impacting the way people work and
how companies are adapting to a world that is
increasingly characterized by automation and
digital transformation.

It begins with an overview of the current state of
the job market and how digital transformation is
affecting it. It then delves into the impact of the
internet and digital technology on the labor
force, from how it is changing the way people

seek and find employment to how it is creating new opportunities for people. It also looks at the challenges faced by companies in adapting to these changes, from hiring and retaining talent to managing the changing workforce.

The End of Jobs concludes with a look at how companies can remain competitive in a rapidly changing job market. It offers advice on how businesses can use technology to remain agile and ensure they can capitalize on the opportunities presented by digital transformation. Overall, It provides an insightful and comprehensive view of the changes in the labor market, the challenges companies face, and how they can remain competitive in an ever-evolving job market.

Conclusion

From Zero to One is an exploration of the forces
that shape the world of business and finance. It
is a book that speaks to the power of creativity
and the potential of the individual. It emphasizes
the importance of having a clear vision and an
understanding of how the world works. It
inspires readers to think outside the box and to
be bold in their approach to business.

The book exhorts people to take chances and
pursue their goals. It also encourages them to be
flexible in their approach to business and to be
open to change. It emphasizes the importance of
developing a solid foundation and thinking
through their decisions before taking action.

At its core, From Zero to One is a book about
the power of the individual. It is a book that
encourages readers to dream big and to take
action. It is a book that emphasizes the
importance of being passionate and creative. It is

a book that encourages readers to take risks and to think outside the box.

Overall, From Zero to One is a book that is both inspirational and informative. It speaks to the power of creativity and the potential of the individual. It provides readers with a roadmap to success and encourages them to be bold and take risks. It is a book that will help readers achieve their goals and to realize their dreams.

www.ingramcontent.com/pod-product-compliance
Lightning Source LLC
Chambersburg PA
CBHW072239230526

45466CB00025B/2191